Hugh Jackman Quiz Book

101 Trivia Questions to Test Your Knowledge of an Entertainment Icon

Nathan MacNeil

Dedication

This book is lovingly dedicated to Hugh Jackman - a remarkable artist and a true inspiration. His dedication to his craft, unwavering commitment to excellence, and his generous spirit both on and off the screen have touched the hearts of millions.

To the fans of Hugh Jackman, whose enthusiasm and love for his work have made this journey all the more meaningful. Your passion has been a guiding light in the creation of this book.

And to all who find joy and inspiration in the arts, may this book remind you of the power of dedication, talent, and hard work in achieving one's dreams.

Table of Contents

Introduction

Step right up to 'Hugh Jackman Quiz Book'! Forget a conventional, linear biography; we're taking a route filled with fun, excitement, and discovery – all in the form of trivia! This book is not just about unearthing facts; it's about celebrating the journey of a man whose talents have dazzled us on the big screen, on stage, and beyond.

Hugh Jackman is a name synonymous with versatility and charisma. From his iconic portrayal of Wolverine to his mesmerizing performances in Broadway musicals, he has shown an incredible range that captivates audiences worldwide. But how well do you know Hugh? Beyond the spotlight and the applause lies a story of a man who is as extraordinary off-screen as he is on it. This book invites you to explore that story, not through lengthy paragraphs or a traditional biography, but through a series of engaging, thought-provoking trivia questions that paint a vivid picture of Hugh's life and career.

Why opt for trivia? Because Hugh Jackman's life is anything but ordinary, it deserves to be explored in a way that's as entertaining and dynamic as he is. Through these trivia questions, we dive into the nuances of his film roles, the anecdotes from his stage performances, the little-known facts about his personal life, and the passions that drive him. It's a journey through the remarkable milestones of his career, the values he stands for, and the diverse roles he's embraced.

As you turn each page, you'll be challenged and amused and gain a deeper appreciation for Hugh's journey from an Australian TV actor to a global superstar. This book is more than just a trivia quiz; it's a celebration of a man who has redefined what it means to be an entertainer and a humanitarian.

So, get ready to embark on an adventure as unconventional and thrilling as Hugh Jackman's career. Whether you're a die-hard fan or just discovering the magic of 'Hugh Jackman Quiz Book' is your ticket to an unforgettable exploration. Let's begin this exciting journey and discover the many facets of a true showman. Welcome aboard!

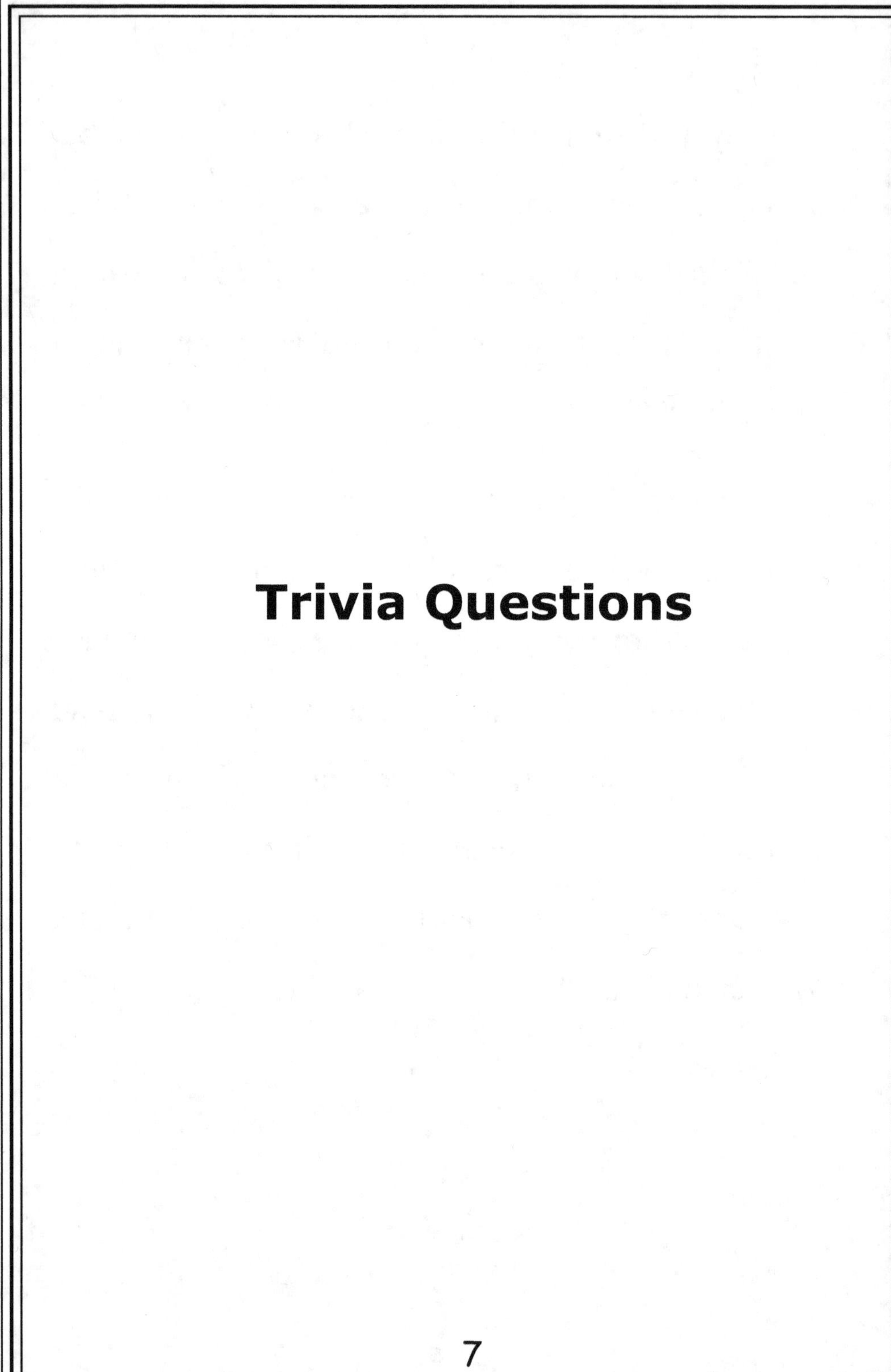

Trivia Questions

1. In which country was Hugh Jackman born?

    A) United States

    B) United Kingdom

    C) Australia

    D) New Zealand

2. Which character in the X-Men series is Hugh Jackman best known for playing?

    A) Professor X

    B) Cyclops

    C) Wolverine

    D) Magneto

3. Which Broadway musical earned Hugh Jackman a Tony Award in 2004?

    A) Oklahoma!

    B) The Phantom of the Opera

    C) The Boy from Oz

D) Chicago

4. What is the name of Hugh Jackman's wife?

A) Deborra-Lee Furness

B) Nicole Kidman

C) Michelle Williams

D) Anne Hathaway

5. Which major awards ceremony has Hugh Jackman hosted?

A) The Grammys

B) The Oscars

C) The Emmys

D) The Tonys

6. In which film did Hugh Jackman play a rugged frontiersman opposite Nicole Kidman?

A) Van Helsing

B) Australia

C) The Prestige

D) Swordfish

7. Hugh Jackman voiced a character in which animated film?

A) Madagascar

B) Zootopia

C) Rise of the Guardians

D) Happy Feet

8. For which film did Hugh Jackman undergo a significant physical transformation, bulking up considerably?

A) Les Misérables

B) The Greatest Showman

C) Prisoners

D) Logan

9. What was Hugh Jackman's profession before he became an actor?

A) Teacher

B) Journalist

C) Personal Trainer

D) Lawyer

10. Hugh Jackman is a global ambassador for which organization?

A) UNICEF

B) World Vision

C) Red Cross

D) Oxfam

11. In which stage production did Hugh Jackman play the role of Gaston?

A) Les Misérables

B) The Phantom of the Opera

C) Beauty and the Beast

D) The Boy from Oz

12. For which movie did Hugh Jackman receive his first Academy Award nomination?

A) The Prestige

B) Les Misérables

C) Prisoners

D) Logan

13. What was Hugh Jackman's first major TV role in Australia?

A) Correlli

B) Neighbours

C) Home and Away

D) Underbelly

14. In "The Greatest Showman," which historical figure did Jackman play the role of?

A) P.T. Barnum

B) Andrew Carnegie

C) Thomas Edison

D) Harry Houdini

15. What is the number of children that Hugh Jackman and Deborra-Lee Furness have??

A) One

B) Two

C) Three

D) None

16. In "Logan," Hugh Jackman's character Wolverine struggles with:

A) Loss of his powers

B) Amnesia

C) An evil twin

D) Time travel

17. Which character did Hugh Jackman portray in the Broadway show "The Music Man"?

    A) Harold Hill

    B) Marcellus Washburn

    C) Tommy Djilas

    D) Mayor Shinn

18. Which film features Hugh Jackman as a character named Robert Angier?

    A) Van Helsing

    B) The Fountain

    C) The Prestige

    D) Real Steel

19. Hugh Jackman is known for following which kind of workout regime for his role as Wolverine?

    A) Yoga and Pilates

    B) CrossFit

C) Weightlifting and High-Intensity Interval Training

D) Marathon Running

20. Hugh Jackman holds a Guinness World Record for what?

A) Most extended duration as a live-action Marvel superhero.

B) Highest-grossing movie musical

C) Most Broadway tickets sold in one day

D) Longest on-screen kiss

21. Hugh Jackman has worked with which director on multiple films, including "The Wolverine" and "Logan"?

A) Darren Aronofsky

B) Baz Luhrmann

C) James Mangold

D) Christopher Nolan

22. In "Eddie the Eagle," Hugh Jackman plays a character who is a:

A) Ski jumper

B) Downhill skier

C) Ski jumping coach

D) Hockey player

23. Which character did Hugh Jackman play in the 2012 "Les Misérables" film adaptation?

A) Marius

B) Javert

C) Enjolras

D) Jean Valjean

24. In which animated film did Hugh Jackman voice a character named Memphis?

A) Zootopia

B) Happy Feet

C) The Croods

D) Kung Fu Panda

25. Which historical figure did Hugh Jackman portray in the musical "The Boy from Oz"?

A) Elton John

B) Peter Allen

C) Frank Sinatra

D) Bob Fosse

26. For which movie did Hugh Jackman receive a Golden Globe Award?

A) The Greatest Showman

B) Les Misérables

C) Prisoners

D) Eddie the Eagle

27. In "Real Steel," Hugh Jackman plays a former boxer involved with what sport?

A) Mixed Martial Arts

B) Robot Boxing

C) Street Racing

D) Wrestling

28. Hugh Jackman played a real-life U.S. senator in which film?

A) The Front Runner

B) J. Edgar

C) The Greatest Showman

D) Prisoners

29. In which movie did Hugh Jackman play a character who travels through time?

A) The Prestige

B) The Fountain

C) Van Helsing

D) X-Men: Days of Future Past

30. Hugh Jackman met his wife, Deborra-Lee Furness, on the set of which TV show?

A) Halifax f.p.

B) Corelli

C) Neighbours

D) The Man from Snowy River

31. Hugh Jackman's character Wolverine is a part of which superhero team in the movies?

A) The Avengers

B) Justice League

C) X-Men

D) Fantastic Four

32. In the film "Prisoners," Hugh Jackman plays a character who is:

A) A detective

B) A superhero

C) A desperate father

D) A professional athlete

33. Hugh Jackman performed at the opening ceremony of which major sporting event?

A) 2000 Sydney Olympics

B) 2008 Beijing Olympics

C) 2012 London Olympics

D) 2016 Rio Olympics

34. Which of these plays featured Hugh Jackman in a leading role on Broadway?

A) The River

B) Death of a Salesman

C) Angels in America

D) The Iceman Cometh

35. Hugh Jackman and this actress have starred together in multiple films, including "Australia" and "Happy Feet":

A) Charlize Theron

B) Nicole Kidman

C) Reese Witherspoon

D) Kate Winslet

36. In the animated movie "Flushed Away," Hugh Jackman voices a character named:

A) Roddy

B) Sid

C) The Toad

D) Le Frog

37. Which song did Hugh Jackman perform in "The Greatest Showman"?

A) "A Million Dreams"

B) "This Is Me"

C) "From Now On"

D) "The Greatest Show"

38. In "Van Helsing," Hugh Jackman plays a character who is a:

A) Vampire

B) Monster Hunter

C) Werewolf

D) Ghost

39. Hugh Jackman is known for his love of which sport?

A) Basketball

B) Rugby

C) Golf

D) Soccer

40. Hugh Jackman supports Laughing Man Foundation, which focuses on:

A) Providing education for children

B) Supporting coffee farmers

C) Animal conservation

D) Fighting climate change

41. Hugh Jackman stars in "The Prestige," a film that primarily falls under which genre?

A) Comedy

B) Science Fiction

C) Historical Drama

D) Thriller

42. Hugh Jackman performed a memorable opening number at the Oscars in which year?

A) 2009

B) 2011

C) 2013

D) 2015

43. Which actress played Hugh Jackman's daughter in the film "Logan"?

A) Dafne Keen

B) Elle Fanning

C) Hailee Steinfeld

D) Mackenzie Foy

44. Hugh Jackman played the role of Billy Bigelow in which musical's concert performance?

A) Carousel

B) Oklahoma!

C) The Music Man

D) South Pacific

45. In which film does Hugh Jackman play a character named Charlie Kenton?

A) Chappie

B) Real Steel

C) Swordfish

D) The Fountain

46. Hugh Jackman practices which form of meditation?

A) Vipassana

B) Transcendental Meditation

C) Zen

D) Mindfulness

47. Hugh Jackman starred in a Broadway production of which musical in 2020?

A) The Boy from Oz

B) The Music Man

C) Les Misérables

D) Chicago

48. One of Hugh Jackman's first acting roles was in a stage production of which Shakespeare play?

A) Macbeth

B) Romeo and Juliet

C) Hamlet

D) A Midsummer Night's Dream

49. To bulk up for his role as Wolverine, Hugh Jackman famously followed a diet that included eating how many meals a day?

A) 3

B) 5

C) 6

D) 8

50. In the animated feature "Missing Link," Hugh Jackman voices a character who is:

A) An explorer

B) A scientist

C) A monster

D) A detective

51. Hugh Jackman's character in the X-Men series, Wolverine, is known for his:

A) Telepathic powers

B) Shape-shifting abilities

C) Metal claws

D) Super speed

52. In the film "Les Misérables," Hugh Jackman's character is pursued by a policeman named:

A) Marius

B) Enjolras

C) Javert

D) Thénardier

53. Hugh Jackman worked with which actress in both "Les Misérables" and "The Greatest Showman"?

A) Zendaya

B) Michelle Williams

C) Anne Hathaway

D) Rebecca Ferguson

54. Hugh Jackman's one-man show, which toured around the world, is titled:

A) Hugh Jackman: Back on Broadway

B) Hugh Jackman: The Man. The Music. The Show.

C) Hugh Jackman: Broadway to Oz

D) Hugh Jackman: Live in Concert

55. Hugh Jackman's first major film role was in:

A) X-Men

B) Swordfish

C) Kate & Leopold

D) Someone Like You

56. Hugh Jackman has hosted the Tony Awards how many times?

A) Once

B) Twice

C) Three times

D) Four times

57. In "The Fountain," Hugh Jackman plays a character in search of:

A) A lost city

B) Immortality

C) A magical sword

D) His true identity

58. In "Chappie," Hugh Jackman plays a character in a film that is primarily a:

A) Romantic Comedy

B) Historical Drama

C) Science Fiction

D) Horror

59. In his early acting career, Hugh Jackman played Gaston in a stage production of:

A) Les Misérables

B) Oklahoma!

C) Beauty and the Beast

D) The Music Man

60. Hugh Jackman is an avid fan of which sports team?

A) New York Yankees

B) Manchester United

C) Australian Wallabies

D) Los Angeles Lakers

61. Which movie features Hugh Jackman in the role of a character named Leopold?

A) Australia

B) Kate & Leopold

C) The Fountain

D) Van Helsing

62. Hugh Jackman co-founded Laughing Man Coffee to support:

A) Education for children in developing countries

B) Environmental conservation

C) Farmers and their communities

D) Performing arts scholarships

63. In "The Prestige," Hugh Jackman's character is obsessed with:

A) Time travel

B) Creating the perfect magic trick

C) Winning a duel

D) Finding lost treasure

64. Hugh Jackman voiced the character of Sir Lionel Frost in which animated film?

A) Zootopia

B) The Croods

C) Missing Link

D) Rise of the Guardians

65. Which character did Hugh Jackman portray in the Broadway show "A Steady Rain"?

A) Denny

B) Joey

C) Ralph

D) Mike

66. Which film did Hugh Jackman star alongside Christian Bale?

A) The Prestige

B) Les Misérables

C) Prisoners

D) The Fountain

67. In the theatrical production "The Boy from Oz," Hugh Jackman played the role of:

A) Liza Minnelli's husband

B) A famous Australian singer-songwriter

C) A Broadway producer

D) A jazz musician

68. Hugh Jackman's acting career began with which type of performance?

A) Television commercials

B) Stage plays

C) Music videos

D) Radio dramas

69. For his Wolverine physique, what type of workout did Hugh Jackman often do?

A) Swimming and cycling

B) Yoga and pilates

C) Heavy weightlifting

D) Long-distance running

70. Hugh Jackman and his wife adopted children from which country?

A) Australia

B) United States

C) Canada

D) United Kingdom

71. Hugh Jackman played the role of Wolverine for the first time in what year?

A) 1999

B) 2000

C) 2001

D) 2002

72. In "Les Misérables," which song does Hugh Jackman's character famously sing?

A) "I Dreamed a Dream"

B) "On My Own"

C) "Bring Him Home"

D) "One Day More"

73. Hugh Jackman received a Golden Globe for Best Actor for his role in:

A) The Greatest Showman

B) Les Misérables

C) Prisoners

D) Eddie the Eagle

74. Before his breakout role in X-Men, Hugh Jackman starred in an Australian TV series called:

A) Correlli

B) Neighbours

C) Home and Away

D) Sea Patrol

75. Hugh Jackman played which role in the stage production of "Oklahoma!"?

A) Curly McLain

B) Jud Fry

C) Will Parker

D) Ali Hakim

76. "Real Steel," starring Hugh Jackman, is a film that combines elements of:

A) Science fiction and sports drama

B) Historical epic and romance

C) Fantasy and musical

D) Horror and comedy

77. In which Broadway musical did Hugh Jackman play the role of Peter Allen?

A) The Boy from Oz

B) Chicago

C) Cabaret

D) Jersey Boys

78. In the film "Prisoners," Hugh Jackman portrays a character who is a:

A) Police detective

B) Criminal mastermind

C) Kidnapped child's father

D) Lawyer

79. Hugh Jackman follows which form of meditation, a technique he's spoken about in interviews?

A) Vipassana

B) Transcendental Meditation

C) Zen

D) Kundalini Yoga

80. Hugh Jackman holds a degree in:

A) Drama

B) Journalism

C) Communications

D) Business Administration

81. Who was the character portrayed by Hugh Jackman in the Royal National Theatre's staging of "Oklahoma!" in 1998?

A) Curly McLain

B) Jud Fry

C) Will Parker

D) Ali Hakim

82. In the animated movie "Happy Feet," Hugh Jackman voices a character who is:

A) A penguin named Memphis

B) A seal named Sven

C) A walrus named Wally

D) An albatross named Al

83. Which famous song does Hugh Jackman's character perform in "The Greatest Showman"?

A) "A Million Dreams"

B) "Come Alive"

C) "The Other Side"

D) "From Now On"

84. Hugh Jackman starred in the film adaptation of which famous musical set in France?

A) The Phantom of the Opera

B) Moulin Rouge!

C) Les Misérables

D) Miss Saigon

85. Hugh Jackman hosted the Tony Awards for the first time in which year?

A) 2003

B) 2004

C) 2005

D) 2006

86. What was Hugh Jackman's first Hollywood movie?

A) X-Men

B) Swordfish

C) Someone Like You

D) Kate & Leopold

87. In "The Fountain," Hugh Jackman's character is involved in a quest for:

A) A cure for cancer

B) A lost treasure

C) Immortality

D) His kidnapped family

88. "Chappie," featuring Hugh Jackman, is primarily a:

A) Romantic comedy

B) Historical drama

C) Science fiction film

D) Horror movie

89. Which character did Hugh Jackman portray in the stage production of "The Boy from Oz"?

A) Peter Allen

B) Elton John

C) Freddie Mercury

D) George Michael

90. Which sport is Hugh Jackman known to be a fan of?

A) Cricket

B) Rugby

C) Soccer

D) Basketball

91. Hugh Jackman and which director worked together on "Australia" and "The Great Gatsby"?

A) Darren Aronofsky

B) Baz Luhrmann

C) Christopher Nolan

D) James Mangold

92. For which role did Hugh Jackman receive his first Emmy Award nomination?

A) Hosting the Oscars

B) Hosting the Tonys

C) His performance in "The Boy from Oz"

D) His guest appearance on "Saturday Night Live"

93. In "The Music Man" on Broadway, Hugh Jackman plays the role of:

A) Harold Hill

B) Marcellus Washburn

C) Mayor Shinn

D) Winthrop Paroo

94. In "Swordfish," Hugh Jackman plays a character who is a:

A) Spy

B) Computer hacker

C) Detective

D) Bank robber

95. Hugh Jackman voiced the character Bunny in which animated film?

A) Rise of the Guardians

B) Happy Feet

C) Madagascar

D) Zootopia

96. Hugh Jackman and his wife Deborra-Lee Furness met while working on which television show?

A) "Correlli"

B) "Neighbours"

C) "Home and Away"

D) "Blue Heelers"

97. One of Hugh Jackman's first professional acting roles was in a production of which musical?

A) "Beauty and the Beast"

B) "Grease"

C) "West Side Story"

D) "Cats"

98. Hugh Jackman hosted the Academy Awards in which year?

A) 2008

B) 2009

C) 2010

D) 2011

99. Which film did Hugh Jackman play the character of Blackbeard in?

A) "Pan"

B) "Hook"

C) "Pirates of the Caribbean"

D) "Treasure Island"

100. In the film "The Greatest Showman," Hugh Jackman portrays:

A) A circus ringmaster

B) A Broadway producer

C) A magician

D) A jazz musician

101. In "Les Misérables," Hugh Jackman's character, Jean Valjean, is known for his:

A) Incredible strength

B) Magical powers

C) Detective skills

D) Musical talent

102. Hugh Jackman won a Tony Award for his portrayal of Peter Allen in "The Boy from Oz." Peter Allen was primarily known as a:

A) Playwright

B) Composer and lyricist

C) Actor and director

D) Dancer and choreographer

103. In which film did Hugh Jackman play a supporting role alongside Christian Bale and Michael Caine?

A) "X-Men"

B) "The Prestige"

C) "Van Helsing"

D) "Swordfish"

104. How many separate films (including cameos) does Hugh Jackman's portrayal of Wolverine span?

A) 5

B) 7

C) 9

D) 11

105. In "Flushed Away," Hugh Jackman voices Roddy, a character who is a:

A) Streetwise rat

B) Domesticated rat

C) Sewer alligator

D) Adventurous mouse

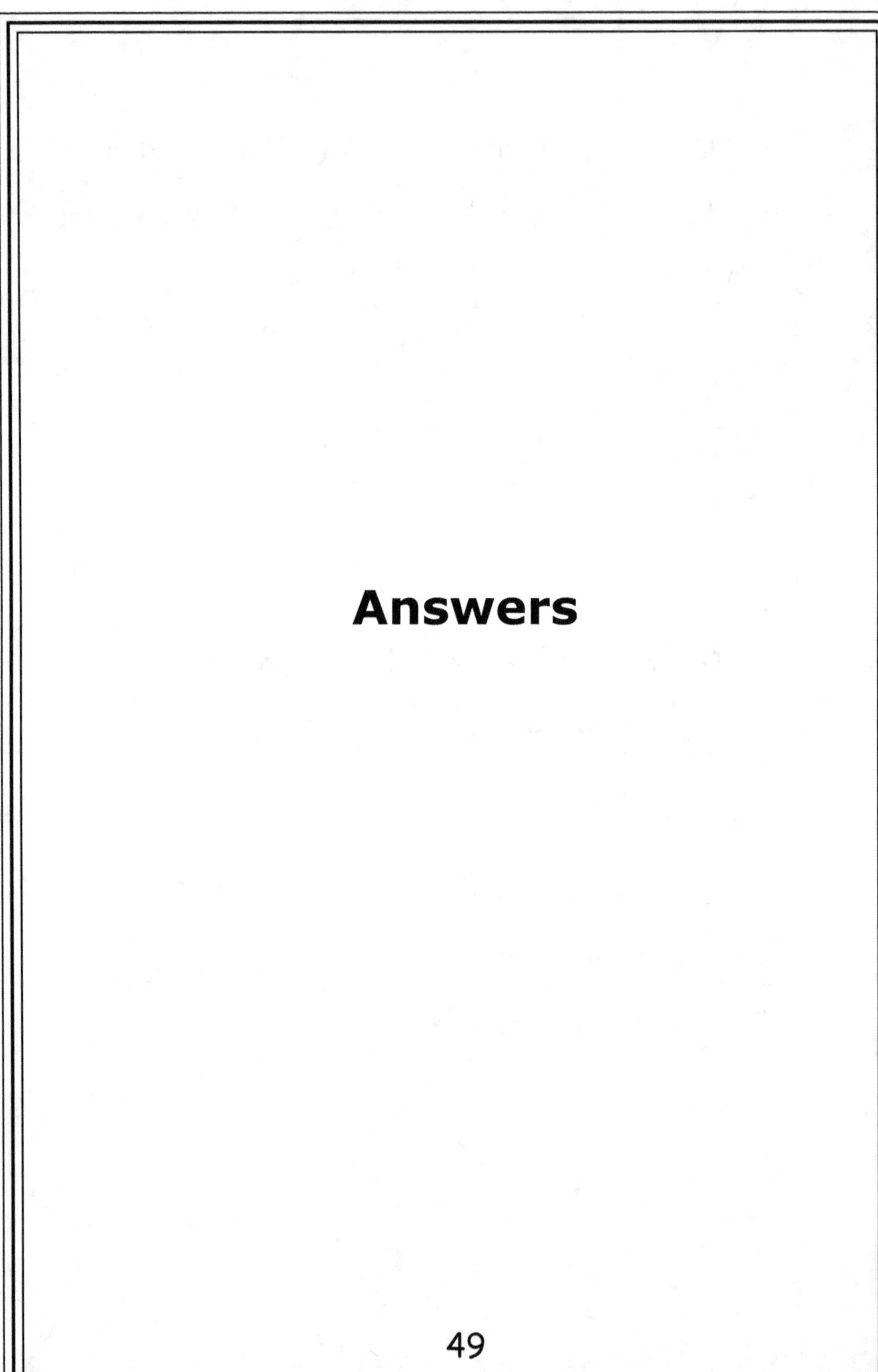

Answers

1. **Country of Birth:** C) Australia

2. **Best Known X-Men Character:** C) Wolverine

3. **Tony Award 2004 Musical:** C) The Boy from Oz

4. **Hugh Jackman's Wife:** A) Deborra-Lee Furness

5. **Awards Ceremony Hosted:** B) The Oscars

6. **Film as a Rugged Frontiersman:** B) Australia

7. **Animated Film Voiced In:** C) Rise of the Guardians

8. **Film with Significant Physical Transformation:** D) Logan

9. **Profession Before Acting:** A) Teacher

10. **Global Ambassador for Organization:** B) World Vision

11. **Role of Gaston in Stage Production:** C) Beauty and the Beast

12. **First Academy Award Nomination:** B) Les Misérables

13. **First Major TV Role in Australia:** A) Correlli

14. **Historical Figure in 'The Greatest Showman':** A) P.T. Barnum

15. **Number of Children:** B) Two

16. **Wolverine's Struggle in 'Logan':** A) Loss of his powers

17. **Character in 'The Music Man':** A) Harold Hill

18. **Character Named Robert Angier:** C) The Prestige

19. **Workout Regime for Wolverine Role:** C) Weightlifting and High-Intensity Interval Training

20. **Guinness World Record Held:** A) Longest career as a live-action Marvel superhero

21. **Director Worked With on Multiple Films:** C) James Mangold

22. **Role in 'Eddie the Eagle':** C) Ski jumping coach

23.**Character in 2012 'Les Misérables'**: D) Jean

Valjean

24.**Voiced Character Named Memphis in**: B) Happy Feet

25.**Historical Figure in 'The Boy from Oz'**: B) Peter

Allen

26.**Golden Globe Award for Movie**: B) Les Misérables

27.**Role in 'Real Steel'**: B) Robot Boxing

28.**Played a Real-Life U.S. Senator in**: A) The Front

Runner

29.**Time Travel Character in Movie**: B) The Fountain

30.**Met Wife on TV Show**: B) Corelli

31. **Superhero Team Wolverine is Part Of**: C) X-Men

32.**Role in 'Prisoners'**: C) A desperate father

33.**Opening Ceremony Performance at Sporting Event**:

A) 2000 Sydney Olympics

34.**Leading Role on Broadway Play:** A) The River

35.**Actress Starred With in Multiple Films:** B) Nicole

Kidman

36.**Voiced Character in 'Flushed Away':** A) Roddy

37.**Song Performed in 'The Greatest Showman':** C)

"From Now On"

38.**Character in 'Van Helsing':** B) Monster Hunter

39.**Sport Hugh Jackman is Known For Loving:** B) Rugby

40.**Focus of Laughing Man Foundation:** B) Supporting

coffee farmers

41. **Genre of 'The Prestige':** D) Thriller

42.**Year of Oscar Opening Number Performance:** A)

2009

43.**Actress Played Daughter in 'Logan':** A) Dafne Keen

44.**Role of Billy Bigelow in Musical's Concert:** A) Carousel

45.**Character Named Charlie Kenton in:** B) Real Steel

46.**Form of Meditation Practiced:** B) Transcendental Meditation

47.**Broadway Musical Starred in 2020:** B) The Music Man

48.**First Acting Role in Shakespeare Play:** D) A Midsummer Night's Dream

49.**Number of Meals a Day for Wolverine Diet:** C) 6

50.**Character in 'Missing Link':** A) An explorer

51. **Wolverine's Known Feature in X-Men Series:** C) Metal claws

52.**Policeman Pursuing His Character in 'Les Misérables':** C) Javert

53. **Actress Worked With in Two Movies:** C) Anne Hathaway

54. **Title of One-Man Show:** B) Hugh Jackman: The Man. The Music. The Show.

55. **First Major Film Role:** A) X-Men

56. **Number of Times Hosted the Tony Awards:** D) Four times

57. **Character's Quest in 'The Fountain':** B) Immortality

58. **Genre of Film 'Chappie':** C) Science Fiction

59. **Played Gaston in Stage Production of:** C) Beauty and the Beast

60. **Favorite Sports Team:** C) Australian Wallabies

61. **Role of Character Named Leopold:** B) Kate & Leopold

62. **Co-Founded Laughing Man Coffee for**: C) Farmers

and their communities

63. **Obsession of Character in 'The Prestige'**: B)

Creating the perfect magic trick

64. **Voiced Sir Lionel Frost in**: C) Missing Link

65. **Portrayed Character in 'A Steady Rain'**: A) Denny

66. **Starred Alongside Christian Bale in**: A) The Prestige

67. **Role in 'The Boy from Oz'**: B) A famous Australian

singer-songwriter

68. **Type of Performance Began Acting Career With**: B)

Stage plays

69. **Type of Workout for Wolverine Physique**: C) Heavy

weightlifting

70. **Country Children Were Adopted From**: B) United

States

71. **First Played Wolverine in Year:** B) 2000

72. **Famous Song Sung in 'Les Misérables':** C) "Bring Him Home"

73. **Golden Globe for Best Actor in:** B) Les Misérables

74. **Australian TV Series Before X-Men:** A) Correlli

75. **Role in Stage Production of 'Oklahoma!':** A) Curly McLain

76. **Elements Combined in 'Real Steel':** A) Science fiction and sports drama

77. **Played Peter Allen in Broadway Musical:** A) The Boy from Oz

78. **Role in 'Prisoners':** C) Kidnapped child's father

79. **Form of Meditation Spoken About in Interviews:** B) Transcendental Meditation

80. **Degree Held In:** C) Communications

81. **Character in Royal National Theatre's 'Oklahoma!':**

A) Curly McLain

82. **Voices Character in 'Happy Feet':** A) A penguin

named Memphis

83. **Famous Song in 'The Greatest Showman':** D) "From

Now On"

84. **Film Adaptation of French Musical Starred In:** C)

Les Misérables

85. **First Hosted Tony Awards in Year:** A) 2003

86. **First Hollywood Movie:** A) X-Men

87. **Character's Quest in 'The Fountain':** C)

Immortality

88. **Genre of 'Chappie':** C) Science Fiction

89. **Portrayed Character in 'The Boy from Oz':** A)

Peter Allen

90.Fan of Which Sport: B) Rugby

91. Director Worked With on 'Australia' and 'The Great Gatsby': B) Baz Luhrmann

92.First Emmy Award Nomination For: B) Hosting the Tonys

93.Role in 'The Music Man' on Broadway: A) Harold Hill

94.Character in 'Swordfish': B) Computer hacker

95.Voiced Bunny in Animated Film: A) Rise of the Guardians

96.Met Wife While Working on TV Show: A) "Correlli"

97.First Professional Acting Role in Musical: B) "Grease"

98.Hosted Academy Awards in Year: B) 2009

99.Played Blackbeard in Film: A) "Pan"

100. **Portrays in 'The Greatest Showman':** A) A circus ringmaster

101. **Known for in 'Les Misérables':** A) Incredible strength

102. **Won Tony Award for Portraying:** B) Composer and lyricist Peter Allen

103. **Supporting Role Alongside Bale and Caine in:** B) "The Prestige"

104. **Number of Films as Wolverine:** C) 9

105. **Voices Roddy, a Character in:** B) Domesticated rat in "Flushed Away"